The Fastest Sales

Year Ever

by

Douglas E. Warrington

The increasing speed of life

Is it just me or do you feel that each week is moving faster and faster? Today the weeks are flying by. The four seasons are here and gone so fast. It just feels like life is moving faster and faster each week. I can hardly believe this week marks the one-year anniversary of the fastest sales year ever.

I have been in sales for over thirty-seven years. Yes, that is a long time and at my age you would think time would be slowing down but no, it is seeding up. I have enjoyed this year more than any other year before. I work with the best people ever and we supply a portfolio of products that truly create real value for the end user. We have a great cost position and high-quality production. What more could you ask for?

Well you could ask for better sales results! I expected

better results… but they are not there. It is even

concerning if I should be considered for termination

from this position based on overall results. I have

failed to reach the sales objective set jointly by me

and my employer. I have in previous sales

management positions terminated sale people for

failure to reach agreed upon results. I know what is

expected, I know what is needed to keep a business

profitable, SALES. I know what a salesperson needs

to deliver to keep a position, SALES.

This has been a fast year that may come to an end

with a sad result.

What have you learned this year?

I ask myself this question, what have you learned this year, last week while driving to my Uncle's funeral. It is interesting how a funeral can make you stop time and reflect. It has always amazed me how a funeral is usually less than a week event from death to burial. So much must be done, so many decisions, so many contacts and final arrangements. During a time of great emotional pain and stress. Yet it gets done and on time to respectfully celebrate a life lived.

During the drive by myself I found the answer to the question, what have you learned this year. The answer has three parts; Relationship, Process, and Target Acquisition.

Relationships. People buy from people – wrong! People buy based on a relationship and it does not have to be another person in the relationship it could be a brand. Buyers have personal relationships and they have brand relationships. A buyer will tell you they buy from X company because they know and trust Bob, but when Bob moves on, they continue to buy from that same company, Why? Because they have created a relationship with the brand, the company, they have a business relationship. Relationships are the most important asset in business. Invest in them personally but also corporately. Build your corporate brand every day through direct customer interaction. I have spent most of this year competing against powerful brand relationships. It takes time and it takes consistency of interaction. It also requires a clear personal branding message. A message that answers the question for your customer; what will you do for me?

I answered that question with; I can lower your cost of a critical business input. The fact proved true even if they did not buy from me. All they had to do was tell their current supplier I was here and show them the price they need to match and boom... I lowered their cost as promised

Process. On average it takes seven no's to get a yes... you can test this. To make the formula work you need to ask <u>why</u> after each no. You need to get enough information to truly understand the <u>why</u> so you can solve for it. Yes, this is handling sales objections 101 but some many skip this step. It feels so elementary it smells so sale-see it looks like a plaid jacket, but it works. Lessoned relearned don't skip the steps. Run the sales process.

New learning in the automated sales world it takes more. It takes twenty-one touches to get a customer to engage in a purchase. Yes, twenty-one. If you are engaging the customer through email or automated marketing touch points plan on twenty-one quality touches as a minimum. I did not know this. I thought my offer was so compelling that if they just saw it, they would be hooked… wrong. I thought sending them twenty-one messages even over time would become some offensive they would never talk to me… wrong. Twenty-one touch points.

Target Acquisition

Who is your customer? Historically my industry has been a three-step distribution model: Manufacture, Distributor, Retailer, End User. In recent years Distributors have been aggressively rolling-up, purchasing Retailers creating a more streamlined distribution model to the end users. With the expiration of key patents Manufactures have been partnering with Distributors through rebate programs to block generics from market access to the end users. Generic defense strategy. My company is a generic manufacture, high quality lower cost, proven products that the industry knows and is familiar with. But who is my target customer? Who writes my company's name on the check?

Historically Manufactures knew Distributors were their customers, Distributors paid Manufactures.

Historically Distributors knew Retailers were their customers, Retailers paid Distributors.

Historically Retailers knew the End User were their customers, End User paid Retailer.

Most Manufactures would engage in a costly push pull strategy through advertising and rebate programs to make the End User aware of the product offering. Product awareness and product availability across the market was the proven model for decades. High price, High cost.

Answer, engage a direct model? Direct to the End User? One step. Low price Low cost. Only if you can create a relationship with enough End Users. It really is a math equation. Number of relationships <u>times</u> expected volume per relationship <u>over</u> time. You cannot overlook the lesson or requirement number one Relationship. Next you must run the process, seven no's face to face or twenty-one touches. This requires people, time and systems.

The solution hit me like a Burlington Northern Fright train from the left at a Texas dirt road crossing. Three step distribution equals three step pricing and we talk to and sell them all.

- Trailer load Direct –price = cost + X %
- Trailer load reload – price = cost + Xx %
- Pallet load – LTL,price = cost + XX %
- Case load – price = cost +XXXx %

Clear, simple and transparent the customer selects what purchase position they want to be in. I just must communicate the offer correctly, consistently, and aggressively. To a wide range of market participants. Build the brand, ride for the brand! Burn that brand into the market.

Content marketing

Oh yes, content marketing is amazing. It has been around for over 100 years and it works. Sales professionals have been using content marketing for ever and it has worked very well. People want information, it was the reason for newspapers, it is the reason we still have tradeshows and conventions, it is the reason cable news has been so successful, and it is also the reason the internet has grown so large so fast. People want information.

Good salespeople lead with information. If you travel with a good salesperson you would observe them providing information all the time and sometimes a little about their product or services. If you travel with a poor salesperson you will observe them providing information about their product or service exclusively. Big difference.

People crave information and the sharing of information is the bridge to relationship development. You can test this with anyone.

Zig Ziglar had a statement that helped to make him very successful; <u>You can get everything in life you want if you will just help enough other people get what they want. Secrets of Closing the Sale (1984).</u> People want information and so do you. So, take the first step and provide information to your customers, fill their bucket up.

The content focus should be on the needs of the customer. Once you have identified the need, information can be presented in a variety of formats, including news, video, white papers, e-books, infographics, email newsletters, case studies, podcasts, how-to guides, question and answer articles, photos, blogs, etc.

Most of these formats are delivered direct through digital means. But all this content can empower your direct sales team with information to build the brand with your customers.

Note: Humour done right is more powerful than you think.

All the money

All the money you will ever need is currently in the hands of your customers. This sounds so intuitive almost to the point of cliché. But it is so true. As a salesperson if you want a raise or even keep getting your current salary you need to get the money for it from your customers. You customers have more money than your current company. Think about that and let it sink in.

I learned a lesson from a venture fund investor a few year ago. He stated that if he could distract the leadership of a start-up away from the customer than he had no interest in investing with that start-up. Meaning if his meetings with leadership took precedent over meeting with customers or if his relationship to management was viewed as more important than the customers relationship, do not invest. Because the investment will only succeed if the company is customer focused. The only way the investment gets a return is with customer cash.

All the money you will ever need is currently in the hands of your customers.

It will all work out.

The Author: Douglas E. Warrington

Lives with his wife of 33 years on their daughter's horse farm in Alabama

A native of Delaware, graduate of the University of Delaware

Blessed to have lived in DE, VA, MI, Ohio, PA and Alabama

Received the MBA from Auburn University

Learned to sell through Dale Carnegie training

Learned to present from Zig Ziglar cassette tapes

Learned to manage a sales team from Larry Huff

Learned to live in freedom through the word of GodIt will all work out.

Website required

I built a website to engage my customers and then I built a website to facilitate ecommerce with my customers. I can tell you firsthand anyone can do this, it took less than a day for each. I also placed my products on Amazon, eBay, Facebook and Google market.

Check it out:

http://aquaticflumi.com/

https://pondweedherbicide.com

https://www.facebook.com/Aquaticflumi

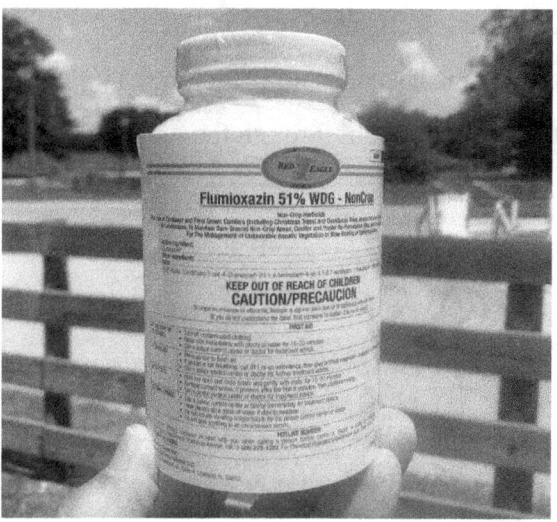

My Product Flumioxazin

Generic Flumioxazin 51% WDG – NonCrop, the NEW option in aquatic and terrestrial plant control.

Flumioxazin 51% WDG – NonCrop provides fast and long-term selective control of some of the toughest and most problematic species in Aquatic and Terrestrial Vegetation Management.

Aquatic:
- Foliar Application Rate 6-12 oz Per Surface Acre, for Full Season Control
- Versatile Subsurface Injection Application Rate 200-400 ppb
- Versatile Contact Herbicide for Controlling Problematic Aquatic Plants
- Excellent Tank Partner for Enhancing Efficacy of Select Aquatic Herbicides
- Dissipates Quickly from Water Column Providing a Favorable Environmental Profile

Terrestrial:
- Low Use Rate – 8-12 oz/acre (24 oz/acre Maximum Annual Rate)
- Broad Spectrum Pre- and Post-Emergent Activity
- Tank Mix Friendly – Compatible with Numerous Other Herbicides
- Resistance Management Tool
- Stays Where It Is Sprayed

Flumioxazin 51% WDG – NonCrop, active ingredient Flumioxazin, an N-phenylphthalimide herbicide. The mode of action in this chemistry family is inhibition of protoporphyringogen oxidase (Protox), an enzyme important in the synthesis of chlorophyll. Formulated as a water dispersible granule, it contains 51% active ingredient of Flumioxazin. Group 14 N-phenylphthalimide.

Flumioxazin 51% WDG-NonCrop is in stock and available now <u>direct</u> from Red Eagle International.

| | GROUP | 14 | HERBICIDE |

Flumioxazin 51% WDG - NonCrop

Non-Crop Herbicide

For Use in Container and Field Grown Conifers (including Christmas Trees) and Deciduous Trees, Around Established Woody Ornamentals in Landscapes, To Maintain Bare Ground Non-Crop Areas, Conifer and Poplar Re-Forestation Sites, and Dormant Turfgrass. For The Management of Undesirable Aquatic Vegetation in Slow Moving or Quiescent Waters.

Active Ingredient:	By Wt.
Flumioxazin*	51%
Other Ingredients:	49%
Total:	100%

*2-[7-fluoro-3,4-dihydro-3-oxo-4-(2-propynyl)-2H-1,4-benzoxazin-6-yl]-4,5,6,7-tetrahydro-1H-isoindole-1,3(2H)-dione

KEEP OUT OF REACH OF CHILDREN
CAUTION/PRECAUCION

Si usted no entiende la etiqueta, busque a alguien para que se la explique a usted en detalle.
(If you do not understand the label, find someone to explain it to you in detail.)

FIRST AID	
IF ON SKIN OR CLOTHING:	• Take off contaminated clothing. • Rinse skin immediately with plenty of water for 15-20 minutes. • Call a poison control center or doctor for treatment advice.
IF INHALED:	• Move person to fresh air. • If person is not breathing, call 911 or an ambulance, then give artificial respiration, preferably by mouth-to-mouth, if possible. • Call a poison control center or doctor for further treatment advice.
IF IN EYES:	• Hold eye open and rinse slowly and gently with water for 15-20 minutes. • Remove contact lenses, if present, after the first 5 minutes, then continue rinsing. • Call a poison control center or doctor for treatment advice.
IF SWALLOWED:	• Call a poison control center or doctor immediately for treatment advice. • Have person sip a glass of water if able to swallow. • Do not induce vomiting unless told to by the poison control center or doctor. • Do not give anything to an unconscious person.

HOTLINE NUMBER

Have the product container or label with you when calling a poison control center or doctor, or going for treatment. For 24 Hour Medical Emergency Assistance (Human or Animal), call **1-800-222-1222** For Chemical Emergency Assistance (Spill, Leak, Fire, or Accident), call CHEMTREC 1-800-424-9300

Manufactured For:
RedEagle International LLC
5143 S. Lakeland Dr., Suite 4, Lakeland, FL 33813

EPA Reg. No.: 85678-35 Net
Contents: 5 Pounds

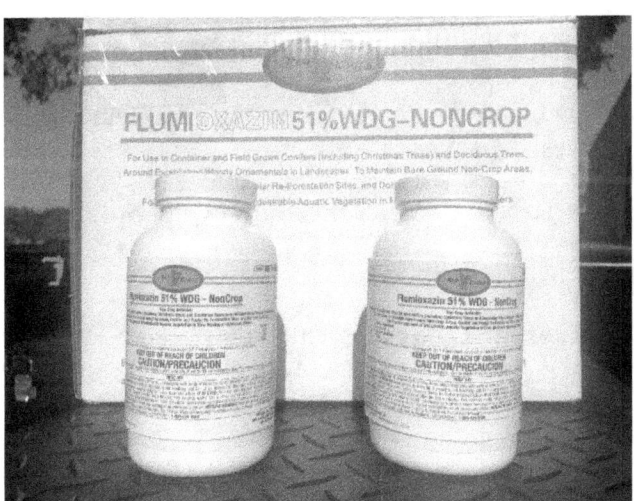

RedEagle
International introduces <u>Generic</u> Flumioxazin 51%
IVM, the new Flumioxazin option for bare ground
weed control. Flumioxazin 51% IVM provides
excellent control of some of the toughest weeds in
industrial vegetation management including kochia,
pigweeds, marestail, and annual grasses.

Flumioxazin 51% IVM

Low Use Rate: 8-
12 oz/acre (24 oz/acre max annual rate)

Broad Spectrum Pre- and Post-
Emergent Weed Control

Long Lasting Residual with No Ground Water Restric
tions

Tank Mix Friendly—
Compatible with other Bare Ground Products

Excellent Control of ALS, Glyphosate and Other Her
bicide Resistant Weeds

Adheres To Soil Particles plus Low Water Solubility

Stays Where It Is Sprayed

Accelerates the Post-Emergent
Herbicidal Activity of Weak Acid Herbicides Such as
 2,4-D Amine, Glyphosate, Dicamba and Others

Group 14 N-phenylphthalimide

The active ingredient Flumioxazin, an N-phenylphthalimide herbicide. The mode of action in this chemistry family is inhibition of protoporphyringogen oxidase (Protox), an enzyme important in the synthesis of chlorophyll. Formulated as a water dispersible granule, it contains 51% active ingredient of Flumioxazin.

Use Tips / For Best Results:

Always use a high-quality Water Conditioner to tie up antagonistic hard water ions present in carrier

Moisture is necessary to move Flumioxazin 51% IVM from the soil surface into soil where weed seeds germinate for residual weed

When applying Flumioxazin 51% IVM after weed emergence, mix with Glyphosate, to aid in initial weed burn. Post emergent applications are most effective when applied under sunny conditions at temperature above 65°F. Flumioxazin 51% IVM is rain fast one hour after application.

Flumioxazin 51% IVM is in stock and available now direct from Red Eagle International.

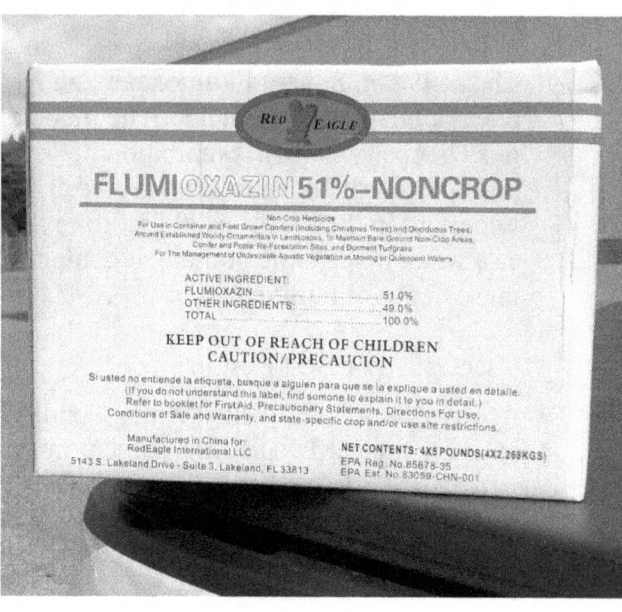

The Standard for Bare-Ground Weed Control...
Flumioxazin 51% IVM from RedEagle International LLC.

Lower cost changes everything... more utilization of a proven chemistry.

ACTIVE INGR.   flumioxazin (51%)
FORMULATION   water-dispersible granule
PACKAGE SIZE   5 x 5 lbs. jugs per case
(20lbs per case)

For specific application rates, directions, mixing instructions and precautions, read the product label.

Please
visit. www.redeagleinternational.com/products/ to
download a full label.

When it comes to keeping railways, roadways and
utility grounds manageable and weed-free,
Flumioxazin 51% IVM (compare to Payload®
Herbicide) succeeds. Flumioxazin 51% IVM delivers
long-lasting, broad-spectrum control and even halts
herbicide-resistant weeds. And, the proven mode of
action of Flumioxazin (same as Payload® Herbicide)
stops tough weeds like kochia, pigweeds, Russian
thistle and more than 100 other bare-ground weeds.

Payload® is a registered trademark of Valent U.S.A.
LLC.

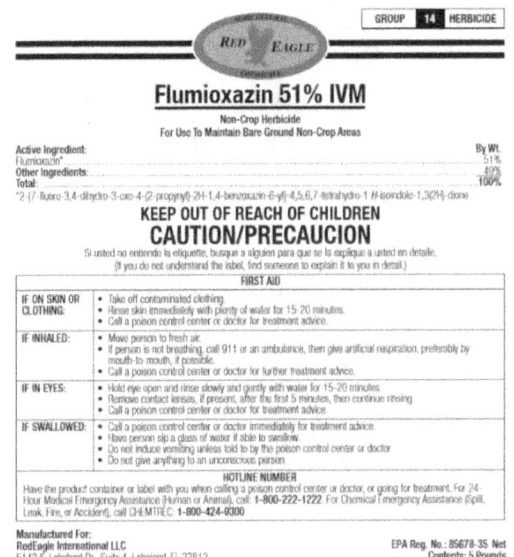

GROUP 14 HERBICIDE

RED EAGLE

Flumioxazin 51% IVM
Non-Crop Herbicide
For Use To Maintain Bare Ground Non-Crop Areas

Active Ingredient:	By Wt.
Flumioxazin*	51%
Other Ingredients:	49%
Total:	100%

*2-[7- fluoro-3,4-dihydro-3-oxo-4-(2-propynyl)-2H-1,4-benzoxazin-6-yl]-4,5,6,7-tetrahydro-1 H-isoindole-1,3(2H)-dione

KEEP OUT OF REACH OF CHILDREN
CAUTION/PRECAUCION
Si usted no entiende la etiqueta, busque a alguien para que se la explique a usted en detalle.
(If you do not understand the label, find someone to explain it to you in detail.)

FIRST AID	
IF ON SKIN OR CLOTHING:	• Take off contaminated clothing. • Rinse skin immediately with plenty of water for 15-20 minutes. • Call a poison control center or doctor for treatment advice.
IF INHALED:	• Move person to fresh air. • If person is not breathing, call 911 or an ambulance, then give artificial respiration, preferably by mouth-to-mouth, if possible. • Call a poison control center or doctor for further treatment advice.
IF IN EYES:	• Hold eye open and rinse slowly and gently with water for 15-20 minutes. • Remove contact lenses, if present, after the first 5 minutes, then continue rinsing. • Call a poison control center or doctor for treatment advice.
IF SWALLOWED:	• Call a poison control center or doctor immediately for treatment advice. • Have person sip a glass of water if able to swallow. • Do not induce vomiting unless told to by the poison control center or doctor • Do not give anything to an unconscious person.

HOTLINE NUMBER
Have the product container or label with you when calling a poison control center or doctor, or going for treatment. For 24-Hour Medical Emergency Assistance (Human or Animal), call 1-800-222-1222 For Chemical Emergency Assistance (Spill, Leak, Fire, or Accident), call CHEMTREC: 1-800-424-9300

Manufactured For:
RedEagle International LLC
5143 S. Lakeland Dr., Suite 4, Lakeland, FL 33813

EPA Reg. No.: 85678-35 Net
Contents: 5 Pounds

Red Eagle Order process

Fast & Simple
Orders Go To: orders@redeagleinternational.com

- Company Name

- PO # (we use this for tracking also)

- Product name

- Quantity

- Price & Terms

- Ship To Location Address

- Billing Email and or Address (we would prefer electronic billing)

Every day we are looking for ways to reduce cost and improve operational efficiency.

- Flumioxazin 51% IVM (the NEW cost-effective standard in the RR market)

- Flumioxazin 51% WDG – NonCrop (full aquatic label)

If you have any questions, please let me know.

Thanks,
Doug Warrington
Business Manager Specialty Products
dwarrington@redeagleinternational.com
Cell: 334-758-1097

Sometimes the best strategy is to use a higher labeled rate, but per-acre costs seem prohibitive. Our lower price gives you the ability to use a higher labeled rate to fight resistant or stubborn weeds without spending more than you already pay.

Industrial Bare Ground option: 8-12 oz. of Flumioxazin 51% IVM could be purchased for less than $13.00 to $19.50 per acre. ($26.00 per lb.)

Flumioxazin 51% IVM

Please always read and follow label directions.

Link to labels on our website:
www.redeagleintenational.com

www.ingramcontent.com/pod-product-compliance
Lightning Source LLC
Chambersburg PA
CBHW072240230526
45466CB00025B/2206